Demyelinating Diseases and Aging

*How to Prevent and Delay
Cognitive Decline*

(Things You Must Know)

Isabella White

About the Book

Demyelinating diseases like multiple sclerosis and transverse myelitis can have devastating effects on the central nervous system, damaging myelin and leading to cognitive impairment. As we age, these effects often compound, causing accelerated cognitive decline and loss of independence.

In this empowering book, leading researcher and health expert Dr. Isabella White draws on the latest scientific research and decades of clinical experience to provide a holistic guide to supporting brain health and delaying cognitive decline. With compassion and expertise, Dr. White explains the neuroscience behind demyelination and age-related changes, arming readers with the knowledge to evaluate their risk factors and symptoms.

Going beyond conventional treatments, this book explores lifestyle strategies—exercise, diet, mental engagement, and stress relief—that can protect myelin and cognition against further deterioration. Dr. White offers adaptable tips to enhance function and outlines emerging therapies that bring hope. Readers are guided through developing a personalized prevention plan while learning when to seek professional support.

Filled with practical advice and inspiring stories, Demyelinating Diseases and Aging enables those diagnosed to take charge of their neurological health. This profoundly insightful book provides the keys to managing symptoms and unlocking one's fullest cognitive potential across their lifespan. Anyone concerned with preserving brain function will find this an indispensable and empowering resource.

Introduction

People diagnosed with demyelinating conditions like multiple sclerosis, the future can feel daunting and uncertain. _Will symptoms progressively worsen? Will cognition and independence gradually decline?_ These common fears stem from the devastating effects of demyelination on the central nervous system. When myelin, the protective coating around nerve fibers, becomes damaged, our abilities are at risk.

Yet emerging research reveals we have a far greater capacity to influence the trajectory of neurological health than previously realized. Groundbreaking studies show lifestyle factors like exercise, nutrition, cognitive stimulation, and stress reduction can significantly impact myelin regeneration and cognitive resilience. Advances in remyelinating therapies using stem cell modulation, antibody technologies, and gene modifications are even more revolutionary.

In this progressive new book, healthcare expert **Dr. Isabella White** offers reason for hope and a pathway to empowerment for those diagnosed with demyelinating diseases. With expert yet accessible writing, **Dr. White** translates the latest scientific findings on demyelination, aging, and cognition into practical self-care strategies. Through inspirational patient cases, she reveals how personalized lifestyle changes and thoughtful engagement with healthcare providers can optimize quality of life and strengthen mental faculties against decline.

Demyelinating Diseases and Aging provides evidence-based tools to assess your risks, harness neuroplasticity, manage symptoms, and develop a tailored wellness plan. You will learn how food, exercise, mind-body practices, and social connection can profoundly alter genetic expression and neurological functioning.

Dr. White explores assorted vitamins, supplements, and emerging pharmaconutrients that enhance myelin repair and cognitive performance. She also offers wise guidance on navigating your medical team, evaluating alternative therapies, and monitoring changes through cognitive assessments.

This deeply researched yet highly readable book enables those with demyelinating diagnoses to truly master their neurological health, prevent deterioration, and unlock their highest cognitive potential across the lifespan. Even those without demyelinating conditions will gain invaluable insights into maintaining sharpness and function as they age. If you or a loved one want to move beyond coping with a diagnosis into thriving with empowered self-care, this could be the most important book you will read.

Let **Dr. White's** wisdom instill optimism, conviction, and disciplined motivation in you. Take control of your neurological well-being starting today. A fulfilling future awaits those with the knowledge, tools, and determination to delay decline, and this book delivers it all. The journey to a healthier you begins now.

Table of Contents

Chapter 1

Understanding Demyelinating Diseases

What Is Myelin, and Why Is It Important?

Myelin is a substance that covers and protects the nerve fibers in your brain and spinal cord. It is made up of protein and fatty substances, and it forms a layer around the nerve fibers called the myelin sheath. The myelin sheath allows electrical impulses to travel quickly and efficiently along the nerve fibers, enabling communication between different parts of your nervous system and your body.

Myelin is important for many reasons. First, it helps you perform various functions, such as thinking, learning, remembering, moving, sensing, and feeling. Without myelin, these functions would be slower, weaker, or impaired. Second, it helps you maintain your health and well-being. Without myelin, your nerve fibers would be vulnerable to damage, inflammation, and infection. Third, it helps you prevent and delay cognitive decline. Without myelin, your brain would age faster, and you would be more likely to develop neurological disorders such as Alzheimer's disease, Parkinson's disease, and dementia.

Therefore, myelin is essential for your nervous system and your overall health. However, various factors can damage or destroy myelin, such as genetic mutations, autoimmune reactions, infections, toxins, injuries, or aging. When this happens, the nerve fibers lose their insulation and ability to transmit signals properly. This leads to a group of conditions known as demyelinating diseases, affecting millions worldwide.

What Happens in Demyelinating Diseases?

Demyelinating diseases are conditions that cause damage to the protective covering (myelin sheath) that surrounds nerve fibers in your brain, spinal cord, and nerves. The myelin sheath allows electrical impulses to travel quickly and efficiently along the nerve fibers, enabling communication between different parts of your nervous system and your body.

When the myelin sheath is damaged, nerve impulses slow or even stop, causing neurological problems. Depending on which part of the nervous system is affected, demyelinating diseases can cause symptoms such as vision loss, muscle weakness, muscle stiffness and spasms, loss of coordination, change in sensation, walking problems, changes in bladder and bowel function, and cognitive decline.

Common Demyelinating Conditions

Demyelinating conditions are diseases that damage the protective layer of myelin that surrounds the nerve fibers in the brain, spinal cord, and nerves. This impairs the transmission of nerve signals and causes neurological problems. Some of the common demyelinating conditions are:

- **Multiple sclerosis (MS):** A chronic and progressive condition that affects the central nervous system, especially the brain, spinal cord, and optic nerves. It is caused by an autoimmune reaction that attacks the myelin sheath or the cells that produce and maintain it. It can result in multiple areas of scarring (sclerosis) in the nervous system. It can cause symptoms such as vision loss, muscle weakness, muscle stiffness and spasms, loss of coordination, changes in sensation, walking problems, and cognitive decline.

- **Neuromyelitis optica spectrum disorder (NMOSD):** A rare and relapsing condition that affects the central nervous system, especially the optic nerves and spinal cord. It is caused by an autoimmune reaction targeting a specific protein called aquaporin-4, found in the cells that produce and maintain the myelin sheath. It can result in inflammation and demyelination of the optic nerves and spinal cord, leading to vision loss and paralysis.

- **Myelin oligodendrocyte glycoprotein antibody-associated disease (MOGAD):** A rare and inflammatory condition affecting the central nervous system, predominantly the optic nerves and spinal cord. It is caused by an autoimmune reaction that targets a specific protein called myelin oligodendrocyte glycoprotein (MOG), which is found in the cells that produce and maintain the myelin sheath. It can result in inflammatory disorders of the optic nerves and spinal cord, such as optic neuritis and transverse myelitis.

- **Transverse myelitis:** A rare and acute condition that affects the spinal cord. It involves inflammation in the spinal cord that can damage the myelin and leave permanent scars or lesions. It can be caused by various factors, such as infections, autoimmune disorders, or vascular problems. It can cause symptoms such as weakness, numbness, tingling, limb pain, and changes in bladder and bowel function.

- **Guillain-Barré syndrome (GBS):** A rare and acute condition affecting the peripheral nervous system, which connects the brain and spinal cord to the rest of the body. It is caused by an immune system response that mistakenly attacks the myelin sheath of the peripheral nerves. It can result in weakness, numbness, tingling, pain in the limbs, and, in severe cases, respiratory failure.

- **Chronic inflammatory demyelinating polyneuropathy (CIDP):** A rare and chronic condition that affects the peripheral nervous system, similar to GBS, but with a chronic and relapsing course. It is caused by an immune system response that mistakenly attacks the myelin sheath of the peripheral nerves. It can result in weakness, numbness, tingling, and pain in the limbs, and, in some cases, problems with balance, coordination, and vision.

Chapter 2

The Aging Brain and Cognition

Age-Related Changes in Cognition

Cognition is the mental process of acquiring and using knowledge. It involves various abilities, such as memory, attention, reasoning, problem-solving, decision-making, and language. Cognition is essential for everyday functioning and well-being.

As people age, their cognition changes in various ways. Some changes are normal and expected, while others may indicate a problem or disease.

Normal age-related changes in cognition are subtle and mostly affect the speed and efficiency of mental processes. They do not affect the overall intelligence or knowledge of older adults. Some aspects of cognition, such as vocabulary and general knowledge, improve with age.

According to the National Institute on Aging, some of the normal age-related changes in cognition are:

- **Slower reaction times:** Older adults may take longer to respond to stimuli, such as sounds, images, or words. This may affect their performance on tasks that require quick responses, such as driving or playing video games.

- **Reduced problem-solving abilities:** Older adults may have more difficulty solving complex or novel problems, such as puzzles or brain teasers. They may also need help switching between different tasks or strategies.

- **Decreased attention span:** Older adults may have more difficulty focusing on a single task or source of information, especially if there are distractions or interruptions. They may also need help to divide their attention between multiple tasks or sources of information, such as multitasking or following a conversation.

- **Slower information processing:** Older adults may take longer to encode, store, and retrieve information in their memory. This may affect their ability to learn new things, remember names or details, or recall past events.

- **Decline in working memory:** Older adults may have more difficulty holding and manipulating information in their short-term memory, such as remembering a phone number or doing mental arithmetic. Working memory is important for reasoning, planning, and decision-making.

These changes in cognition may affect the daily functioning and quality of life of older adults. For example, they may need help to perform tasks that require speed, accuracy, or complexity, such as managing finances, following instructions, or using technology. They may also affect older adults' social and emotional well-being, such as self-confidence, mood, or relationships. Therefore, older adults and their families need to be aware of these changes in cognition and how to cope with them.

Risk Factors for Cognitive Decline

Cognitive decline is the gradual loss of thinking abilities such as memory, attention, reasoning, and problem-solving. Cognitive decline can affect the daily functioning and quality of life of older adults. Some of the risk factors for cognitive decline include the following:

- **Age:** The risk of cognitive decline increases with age, especially after 65 years old. Age-related changes in the brain, such as reduced blood flow, inflammation, and oxidative stress, can affect the structure and function of the brain cells and the connections between them.

- **Genetics:** Some genes can influence the risk of cognitive decline by increasing or decreasing it. For example, the APOE gene, which is involved in cholesterol metabolism and inflammation, has different variants that can affect the risk of Alzheimer's disease, the most common cause of dementia.

- **Family history:** Having a parent or sibling with cognitive decline or dementia can increase the risk of developing the same condition, especially if the onset was before 65 years old. This may be due to genetic or environmental factors, or both.

- **Medical conditions:** Some chronic or acute medical conditions can affect the brain and increase the risk of cognitive decline. These include diabetes, high blood pressure, high cholesterol, heart disease, stroke, head injury, infections, thyroid problems, kidney disease, and liver disease.

- **Lifestyle factors:** Some habits or behaviors can influence the risk of cognitive decline by protecting or harming the brain. These include physical activity, diet, smoking, alcohol consumption, sleep quality, stress management, social engagement, and cognitive stimulation.

The risk factors for cognitive decline are not deterministic, meaning they do not guarantee that a person will or will not experience cognitive decline. They are probabilistic, meaning that they can increase or decrease the likelihood of cognitive decline.

The Impact of Demyelination on Cognitive Aging

Demyelination is the loss or damage of the protective layer of myelin that surrounds the nerve fibers in the brain and spinal cord. Myelin is essential for the fast and efficient transmission of nerve signals, which underlie various cognitive functions such as memory, attention, reasoning, and problem-solving.

Demyelination can have a negative impact on cognitive aging, as it can impair communication between different brain regions and reduce the brain's plasticity and adaptability. Demyelination can also lead to the degeneration and death of nerve cells, which can cause irreversible brain damage and cognitive decline. Some of the factors that can cause or contribute to demyelination in the aging brain are:

- **Inflammation:** Chronic inflammation in the brain can trigger an immune response that attacks the myelin or the cells that produce and maintain it, such as oligodendrocytes. Inflammation can also disrupt the blood-brain barrier, which protects the brain from harmful substances and infections.

- **Oxidative stress:** Oxidative stress is the imbalance between the production and elimination of reactive oxygen species (ROS), which are molecules that can damage the cells and their components. Oxidative stress can damage the myelin and the mitochondria, which are the cells' energy-producing organelles.

- **Genetics:** Some genetic variants can influence the risk of demyelination and cognitive decline by increasing or decreasing it. For example, the APOE gene, which is involved in cholesterol metabolism and inflammation, has different variants that can affect the risk of Alzheimer's disease, the most common cause of dementia.

- **Lifestyle factors:** Some habits or behaviors can influence the risk of demyelination and cognitive decline by protecting or harming the brain. These include physical activity, diet, smoking, alcohol consumption, sleep quality, stress management, social engagement, and cognitive stimulation.

Chapter 3

Lifestyle Strategies to Protect Myelin and Cognition

Exercise and Activity for Brain Health

Exercise and activity are important for maintaining and improving mental and physical health. Studies have shown that exercise can boost cognition, memory, mood, and well-being and prevent or delay cognitive decline and dementia. _How does exercise benefit your brain?_ Several mechanisms explain the positive effects of exercise on your brain, such as:

- Increasing blood flow and oxygen delivery to the brain enhances the function and survival of brain cells.

- Stimulating the growth of new brain cells and connections, especially in the hippocampus, is responsible for learning and memory.
- Reducing inflammation and oxidative stress can damage the brain cells and the myelin sheath.
- Modulating the levels of neurotransmitters, hormones, and growth factors, which are involved in mood, motivation, and cognition.
- Improving the brain's plasticity and adaptability enables the brain to cope with challenges and changes.

What kind of exercise is good for your brain? The general recommendation is to do at least 150 minutes of moderate-intensity aerobic exercise per week, 75 minutes of vigorous-intensity exercise per week, or a combination of both. Aerobic exercise is any activity that increases your heart rate and breathing, such as walking, jogging, cycling, swimming, or dancing. Aerobic exercise can improve cardiovascular health, which is linked to brain health.

However, aerobic exercise is not the only exercise that can benefit your brain. You should also include muscle-strengthening activities, such as lifting weights, pushing-ups, or using resistance bands, at least twice a week. Muscle-strengthening activities can improve muscle mass, bone density, balance, and coordination, preventing falls and injuries and enhancing mobility and independence.

As part of your routine, consider doing some flexibility and balance exercises, such as stretching, yoga, or tai chi. Flexibility and balance exercises can improve your range of motion, posture, and stability, reducing pain and stiffness and preventing falls and fractures.

The most important thing is to choose an exercise that you enjoy and that suits your abilities and preferences. You can also vary your exercise routine to keep it exciting and challenging. You can also exercise with other people, such as friends, family, or a group, to make it more fun and social.

Anti-Inflammatory Diet and Nutrition

An anti-inflammatory diet and nutrition are essential for your brain health as well as your overall health. Research shows that eating foods that reduce inflammation can help protect your myelin and detect, prevent, or delay cognitive decline and dementia.

How does an anti-inflammatory diet and nutrition benefit your brain? Several mechanisms explain the positive effects of eating anti-inflammatory foods on your brain, such as:

- Providing antioxidants, vitamins, minerals, and phytochemicals that can protect the brain cells and the myelin sheath from oxidative stress and inflammation.
- Modulating fatty acids, cholesterol, glucose, and insulin levels affects brain metabolism and function.
- Supporting the growth and survival of new brain cells and connections, especially in the hippocampus, which is responsible for learning and memory.
- Enhancing the brain's plasticity and adaptability, which enables the brain to cope with challenges and changes.

What kinds of foods are anti-inflammatory? The general recommendation is to eat a balanced and varied diet that includes plenty of fruits, vegetables, whole grains, legumes, nuts, seeds, herbs, spices, and healthy fats and limits processed foods, refined sugars, saturated fats, trans fats, and alcohol. Some of the most anti-inflammatory foods are:

- **Tomatoes:** Tomatoes are rich in lycopene, a powerful antioxidant that can reduce inflammation and protect the brain from oxidative stress.

- **Olive oil**: Olive oil is a good source of monounsaturated fatty acids and polyphenols, which can lower inflammation and improve blood flow to the brain.

- **Green leafy vegetables:** Green leafy vegetables, such as spinach, kale, and collards, are high in vitamin K, folate, and carotenoids, which can protect the brain from inflammation and cognitive decline.

- **Nuts:** Nuts, such as almonds and walnuts, are rich in omega-3 fatty acids, vitamin E, and polyphenols, which can reduce inflammation and oxidative stress in the brain.

- **Fatty fish:** Fatty fish, such as salmon, mackerel, tuna, and sardines, are a great source of omega-3 fatty acids, which can modulate the immune system and protect the myelin and the brain cells from inflammation and damage.

- **Fruits:** Fruits, such as strawberries, blueberries, cherries, and oranges, are loaded with antioxidants, flavonoids, and vitamin C, which can fight inflammation and protect the brain from oxidative stress and aging.

- **Spices:** Spices, such as turmeric, ginger, garlic, and cinnamon, have anti-inflammatory and anti-microbial properties, which can help prevent and treat infections and inflammation in the brain.

An anti-inflammatory diet and nutrition are some of the best things you can do for your brain and overall health. Eating foods that can reduce inflammation protects your myelin and cognition functions and improves your quality of life.

Mental Stimulation and Learning New Skills

Mental stimulation and learning new skills are beneficial for your brain health as well as your overall health. Research has shown that mentally challenging activities can improve your cognition, memory, mood, and well-being and prevent or delay cognitive decline and dementia.

How do mental stimulation and learning new skills benefit your brain? Several mechanisms explain the positive effects of mental stimulation and learning new skills on your brain, such as:

- Enhancing the brain's plasticity and adaptability, which enables the brain to cope with challenges and changes.
- Stimulating the growth of new brain cells and connections, especially in the hippocampus, is responsible for learning and memory.
- Increasing the blood flow and oxygen delivery to the brain enhances the function and survival of brain cells.

- Reducing inflammation and oxidative stress can damage the brain cells and the myelin sheath.
- Modulating the levels of neurotransmitters, hormones, and growth factors, which are involved in mood, motivation, and cognition.

What kind of mental stimulation and learning new skills are good for your brain? The general recommendation is to engage in novel, complex, and enjoyable activities that challenge your mind differently. Some of the examples of mental stimulation and learning new skills are:

- Learning a new language, musical instrument, or hobby.
- Reading books, magazines, or articles on various topics.
- Solving puzzles, crosswords, sudoku, or brain games.
- Taking a course or a class on something that interests you.
- Playing cards, board games, or video games with others.

Mental stimulation and learning new skills are some of the best things you can do for your brain and overall health. By engaging in mentally challenging activities, you can protect your myelin and cognition and improve your quality of life.

Stress Management and Restorative Sleep

Stress management and restorative sleep are essential for your brain health as well as your overall health. Research has shown that managing stress and getting enough quality sleep can help protect your myelin and cognition and prevent or delay cognitive decline and dementia.

How do stress management and restorative sleep benefit your brain? Several mechanisms explain the positive effects of stress management and healthy sleep on your brain, such as:

- Reducing cortisol levels can damage the brain cells and the myelin sheath and impair memory and learning.
- Enhancing the brain's self-repair and regeneration processes, which occur during deep sleep and REM sleep, is important for maintaining and improving brain structure and function.
- Consolidating and integrating new information and memories during sleep is essential for learning and cognition.
- Improving mood and emotional regulation can affect motivation, decision-making, and social interaction.

What are some tips for stress management and restorative sleep? The general recommendation is to adopt healthy habits and routines to help you cope with stress and improve your sleep quality and quantity. Some of the tips are:

- Identify and address the sources of stress in your life, such as work, family, or health issues, and seek professional help if needed.
- Practice relaxation techniques, such as deep breathing, meditation, yoga, or massage, which can lower stress levels and promote calmness and well-being.
- Avoid caffeine, alcohol, nicotine, and other stimulants, especially in the evening, as they can interfere with your sleep and increase your stress levels.
- Establish a regular sleep schedule and stick to it as much as possible, even on weekends and holidays, as this can help your body and mind adjust to a consistent sleep rhythm.
- Create a comfortable and relaxing sleep environment, free of noise, light, and distractions, and use your bed only for sleep and sex, as this can help you associate your bed with rest and intimacy, not with stress and work.
- Avoid using electronic devices, such as phones, computers, or TVs, at least an hour before bedtime, as they can emit blue light that can suppress the

production of melatonin, the hormone that regulates your sleep-wake cycle.

- Engage in physical activity, mental stimulation, and social interaction during the day, as these can help you reduce stress, improve your mood, and make you more tired and ready for sleep at night.

Stress management and restorative sleep are some of the best things you can do for your brain and overall health. Managing stress and getting enough sleep can protect your myelin and cognition and improve your quality of life.

Social and Community Engagement

Social and community engagement are important for your brain health as well as your overall health. Research has shown that being socially connected and involved in your community can enhance your cognition, memory, mood, and well-being and prevent or delay cognitive decline and dementia.

How does social and community engagement benefit your brain? Several mechanisms explain the positive effects of social and community engagement on your brain, such as:

1. Social support can reduce stress, loneliness, and depression and increase self-esteem, happiness, and resilience.

2. Stimulating social cognition involves the mental processes of understanding and interacting with others, such as empathy, perspective-taking, and theory of mind.

3. Enhancing cognitive stimulation, which involves exposure to new and diverse information, ideas, and perspectives, can challenge and enrich your mind.

4. Promoting physical activity can improve cardiovascular health, blood flow, and oxygen delivery to the brain and stimulate the growth of new brain cells and connections.

5. Encouraging healthy behaviors, such as eating a balanced diet, avoiding smoking and excessive alcohol, and getting enough sleep, can protect your brain from inflammation and oxidative stress.

What kind of social and community engagement is good for your brain? The general recommendation is to engage in meaningful, enjoyable, and fulfilling activities involving positive and reciprocal relationships with others. Some of the examples of social and community engagement are:

- Maintaining close and frequent contact with your family and friends and expressing your feelings and needs to them.

- Joining a club, group, or organization that shares your interests, hobbies, or values and participating in their events and activities.
- Volunteering for a cause that you care about and contributing to the well-being of others and society.
- Take a class or a course that teaches you something new and interact with the instructor and the classmates.
- Traveling to new places and experiencing different cultures, languages, and lifestyles.

Social and community engagement are some of the best things you can do for your brain and overall health. Being socially connected and involved in your community can protect your myelin and cognition and improve your quality of life.

Chapter 4

Pharmaceutical and Supplemental Support

Medications for Symptom Management

Medications for symptom management are drugs that can help reduce or relieve the symptoms of demyelinating diseases, such as pain, spasticity, fatigue, bladder problems, and depression. These medications do not cure or modify the disease but can improve the patient's quality of life and functioning.

The type and dosage of medications for symptom management depend on the specific condition, the severity of the symptoms, and the patient's response.

Some of the common medicines for symptom management are:

- **Analgesics:** These painkillers can help ease the pain caused by nerve damage or inflammation. They include nonsteroidal anti-inflammatory drugs (NSAIDs), such as ibuprofen and naproxen, and opioids, such as morphine and oxycodone.
- **Muscle relaxants:** These drugs can help reduce the muscle stiffness and spasms that can affect the movement and posture of the patients. They include baclofen, tizanidine, and diazepam.
- **Fatigue reducers:** These drugs can help improve patients' energy and alertness. They include modafinil, amantadine, and methylphenidate.
- **Bladder modifiers:** These drugs can help control bladder function and prevent urinary tract infections. They include anticholinergics, such as oxybutynin and tolterodine, and beta-3 agonists, such as mirabegron.
- **Antidepressants:** These are drugs that can help improve the mood and emotional well-being of patients. They include selective serotonin reuptake inhibitors (SSRIs), such as fluoxetine and sertraline, and serotonin-norepinephrine reuptake inhibitors (SNRIs), such as duloxetine and venlafaxine.

Medications for symptom management can have side effects, interactions, and contraindications, so they should be used with caution and under medical supervision. Patients should consult their doctors before starting, stopping, or changing any medication and report any adverse reactions or concerns. Patients should also follow the instructions and prescriptions of their doctors and stay within the recommended doses or durations of the medications.

The Use of Vitamins, Herbs and Nutraceuticals

Vitamins, herbs, and nutraceuticals are natural substances that can benefit your health, especially your brain health. Research has shown that some vitamins, herbs, and nutraceuticals can help protect your myelin and cognition and prevent or delay cognitive decline and dementia.

How do vitamins, herbs, and nutraceuticals benefit your brain? Several mechanisms explain the positive effects of vitamins, herbs, and nutraceuticals on your brain, such as:

- Providing antioxidants, vitamins, minerals, and phytochemicals that can protect the brain cells and the myelin sheath from oxidative stress and inflammation.

- Modulating the levels of neurotransmitters, hormones, and growth factors, which are involved in mood, motivation, and cognition.

- Supporting the growth and survival of new brain cells and connections, especially in the hippocampus, which is responsible for learning and memory.

- Enhancing the brain's plasticity and adaptability, which enables the brain to cope with challenges and changes.

What vitamins, herbs, and nutraceuticals are good for your brain? The general recommendation is to eat a balanced and varied diet that includes plenty of fruits, vegetables, whole grains, legumes, nuts, seeds, herbs, spices, and healthy fats and limits processed foods, refined sugars, saturated fats, trans fats, and alcohol. Some of the most beneficial vitamins, herbs, and nutraceuticals for your brain are:

- **Vitamin B12:** Vitamin B12 is essential for the synthesis and maintenance of myelin, as well as the function of nerve cells. A deficiency of vitamin B12 can cause demyelination, nerve damage, and cognitive impairment. Vitamin B12 is mainly found in animal products, such as meat, eggs, and dairy, but it can also be obtained from fortified foods or supplements.

- **Vitamin D:** Vitamin D is important for the immune system and the regulation of inflammation, which can affect the myelin and brain cells. Vitamin D deficiency can increase the risk of demyelinating diseases, such as multiple sclerosis and cognitive decline. When exposed to sunlight, vitamin D is mainly produced by the skin, but it can also be obtained from supplements or foods such as fatty fish, egg yolks, and mushrooms.

- **Omega-3 fatty acids:** Omega-3 fatty acids are essential for the structure and function of the myelin and the brain cells and the modulation of inflammation and oxidative stress. A deficiency of omega-3 fatty acids can impair the myelin and brain function and increase the risk of cognitive decline and dementia. Omega-3 fatty acids are mainly found in fish oil, flaxseed oil, and walnuts but can also be obtained from supplements.

- **Curcumin:** Curcumin is the active ingredient of turmeric, a spice with anti-inflammatory and antioxidant properties. Curcumin can protect the myelin and brain cells from inflammation and oxidative stress and enhance the brain's plasticity and adaptability. Curcumin can be obtained from turmeric powder, capsules, or extracts.

- **Ginkgo biloba:** Ginkgo biloba is an herb used for centuries in traditional medicine. Ginkgo biloba can improve the blood flow and oxygen delivery to the brain and the function and survival of brain cells. Ginkgo biloba can also modulate the levels of neurotransmitters and hormones and improve memory and cognition. Ginkgo biloba can be obtained from leaves, capsules, or extracts.

Vitamins, herbs, and nutraceuticals are some of the options that can help you maintain and improve your brain health, as well as your overall health.

Evaluating the Quality of Supplements

Evaluating the quality of supplements is important for your health, as not all supplements are safe, effective, or reliable. Supplements are not regulated by the FDA in the same way drugs are, so you need to do your own research and be careful when shopping for new products.

Some of the factors that you should consider when evaluating the quality of supplements are:

- **The ingredients:** You should check the supplement's label to see what ingredients it contains, how much of each ingredient it provides, and whether it has any additives, fillers, or allergens. You should also look for the form and source of the ingredients, as some forms may be more bioavailable or potent than others.

- **The claims:** You should be wary of any supplement that makes exaggerated or unrealistic claims, such as curing diseases, reversing aging, or enhancing performance. You should also look for evidence to support the claims, such as scientific studies, testimonials, or certifications. You should avoid any supplement that provides no information or references about its claims.

- **The quality:** You should look for quality indicators, such as seals of approval, third-party testing, or good manufacturing practices. These can help ensure the supplement meets certain purity, potency, and safety standards. However, you should also be aware that some of these indicators may need more reliability and independence and do not guarantee the supplement's effectiveness.

- **Safety:** You should consult your doctor before starting, stopping, or changing supplements and report any adverse reactions or concerns. You should also check for any potential side effects, interactions, or contraindications of the supplement, especially if you have any medical conditions, allergies, or medications. You should also follow your doctor's instructions and prescriptions and not exceed the recommended doses or durations of the supplement.

Chapter 5

Emerging Therapies and Research

Advances in Remyelination Research

Remyelination is the process of repairing or restoring the myelin sheath that surrounds and protects the nerve fibers in the brain and spinal cord. Myelin is essential for the fast and efficient transmission of nerve signals, which underlie various cognitive functions such as memory, attention, reasoning, and problem-solving.

Demyelination is the loss or damage of the myelin sheath, impairing communication between different brain regions and reducing the brain's plasticity and adaptability. Demyelination can also lead to the degeneration and death of nerve cells, which can cause irreversible brain damage and cognitive decline. Demyelination is a hallmark of several neurological disorders, such as multiple sclerosis (MS), neuromyelitis optica spectrum disorder (NMOSD), and chronic inflammatory demyelinating polyneuropathy (CIDP).

These disorders affect millions of people worldwide and have a significant impact on their quality of life and functioning. There is no cure for these disorders, but there are treatments that can help manage the symptoms, modify the course of the disease, and improve the prognosis of the patients. However, these treatments are insufficient to restore the lost or damaged myelin and prevent the progressive neurodegeneration in these disorders.

Therefore, there is a great need for and interest in developing new therapies that promote remyelination and neuroprotection in demyelinating disorders. Remyelination happens naturally and on its own in the brain and spinal cord. It is caused by resident oligodendrocyte precursor cells (OPCs) being recruited and differentiated. OPCs are the cells that make and maintain the myelin sheath.

However, this process is often incomplete and needs to be revised to repair the extensive demyelination in these disorders. The reasons for this remyelination failure are not fully understood, but they may involve factors such as age, inflammation, oxidative stress, genetics, and lifestyle.

In recent years, there have been significant advances in remyelination research, both in understanding the molecular and cellular mechanisms that regulate this process and developing novel strategies and interventions that can enhance this process. Some of the main advances in remyelination research are:

- Identifying and characterizing the factors that influence the proliferation, migration, differentiation, and survival of OPCs, such as growth factors, neurotransmitters, hormones, cytokines, and extracellular matrix components.
- The discovery and validation of new biomarkers and imaging techniques that can measure and monitor the extent and quality of remyelination in vivo, such as magnetic resonance imaging (MRI), positron emission tomography (PET), and optical coherence tomography (OCT).
- The development and optimization of new animal models and in vitro systems that mimic the pathological and physiological conditions of demyelination and remyelination, such as rodent models, zebrafish models, and human-induced pluripotent stem cell (iPSC)-derived models.

- The screening and testing of new pharmacological and non-pharmacological agents that can stimulate or facilitate remyelination, such as small molecules, antibodies, peptides, gene therapies, cell therapies, and electrical stimulation.

These advances in remyelination research have opened new avenues and opportunities for developing effective and safe therapies for demyelinating disorders. However, there are still many challenges and limitations that need to be overcome, such as the translation of preclinical findings into clinical trials, the identification of the optimal timing and duration of the interventions, the evaluation of the long-term outcomes and side effects of the interventions, and the personalization of the interventions according to the individual characteristics and needs of the patients.

Remyelination research is a dynamic and promising field that has the potential to revolutionize the treatment and management of demyelinating disorders. By enhancing the natural ability of the brain and spinal cord to repair and regenerate the myelin sheath, remyelination therapies can improve the function and survival of the nerve cells and, ultimately, the cognition and well-being of patients.

Neuroprotective and Regenerative Treatments

Neuroprotective and regenerative treatments aim to protect the brain cells and the myelin sheath from damage and degeneration and to restore or enhance their function and survival. These treatments can improve the cognition and well-being of patients with demyelinating diseases such as multiple sclerosis, neuromyelitis optica, and chronic inflammatory demyelinating polyneuropathy.

Some of the examples of neuroprotective and regenerative treatments are:

- **Pharmacological agents:** These drugs can modulate the immune system, reduce inflammation, enhance remyelination, or stimulate neurogenesis. Some drugs investigated or tested for neuroprotection and regeneration are fingolimod, siponimod, clemastine, biotin, and metformin.
- **Cell therapies:** These are therapies that involve the transplantation of cells that can produce or repair myelin, such as oligodendrocyte precursor cells (OPCs), mesenchymal stem cells (MSCs), or induced pluripotent stem cells (iPSCs). These cells can also secrete factors that can promote neuroprotection and regeneration.
- **Gene therapies:** These are therapies that involve the delivery of genes that can enhance the function

or survival of the brain cells or the myelin sheath, such as genes that encode growth factors, anti-inflammatory molecules, or myelin proteins. These genes can be delivered by viral or non-viral vectors, such as adeno-associated virus (AAV), lentivirus, or nanoparticles.

- **Electrical stimulation:** This therapy involves applying electrical currents or pulses to the brain or spinal cord, which can modulate the activity and plasticity of the nerve cells and the myelin sheath. This can be done by invasive or non-invasive methods, such as deep brain stimulation (DBS), transcranial magnetic stimulation (TMS), or transcranial direct current stimulation (tDCS).

Neuroprotective and regenerative treatments are promising and innovative therapies that can improve patients' outcomes and quality of life with demyelinating diseases. However, they are still in the early stages of development and face many challenges and limitations, such as the therapies' safety, efficacy, delivery, and personalization.

Chapter 6

Adaptive Strategies to Preserve Cognition

Cognitive Assessment and Tracking Changes

People with demyelinating diseases like multiple sclerosis, neuromyelitis optica, and chronic inflammatory demyelinating polyneuropathy, keeping their minds sharp, testing their cognitive abilities, and keeping track of any changes are crucial. These diseases can affect the brain and spinal cord and cause damage to the myelin sheath that surrounds and protects the nerve fibers.

This can impair the communication between different brain regions and reduce the brain's plasticity and adaptability. This can also lead to the degeneration and death of nerve cells, which can cause irreversible brain damage and cognitive decline.

Cognitive assessment measures and evaluates a person's cognitive abilities and functions, such as memory, attention, reasoning, problem-solving, and language. Cognitive assessment can help identify the strengths and weaknesses of a person's cognition and the presence and severity of any cognitive impairment or dementia. Cognitive assessment can also help monitor the progression and prognosis of the disease and guide the treatment and management of its symptoms.

Cognitive assessment can be done by various methods, such as:

- **Neuropsychological tests:** These are standardized tests that can assess various domains of cognition, such as verbal and visual memory, processing speed, executive function, and verbal fluency. These tests can comprehensively and objectively evaluate a person's cognitive status and profile.
- **Self-report questionnaires:** These can measure a person's subjective perception of their cognitive abilities and functions and the impact of cognitive impairment on their daily activities and quality of life. These questionnaires can provide a

personal and holistic view of a person's cognitive situation and needs.

- **Informant reports:** These are reports that can be obtained from a person's family, friends, or caregivers, who can provide information and feedback on the person's cognitive performance and behavior in real-life situations. These reports can complement and corroborate the results of the other methods.

Cognitive assessment should be done regularly and periodically, as cognitive impairment and dementia can change over time, depending on the course and stage of the disease, as well as other factors such as age, health, and lifestyle. Cognitive assessment should also be done by a qualified and experienced professional, such as a neurologist, a neuropsychologist, or a psychiatrist, who can interpret the results and provide recommendations and referrals.

Tracking changes is the process of recording and analyzing the cognitive assessment results over time and comparing them with the baseline and normative data. Tracking changes can help detect and quantify changes or trends in a person's cognition, such as improvement, stability, or decline. Tracking changes can also help evaluate the effectiveness and safety of any interventions or treatments that aim to preserve or enhance cognition, such as medications, supplements, or lifestyle modifications.

Tracking changes can be done by various methods, such as:

- **Charts and graphs:** These are visual representations that can display the scores and outcomes of the cognitive assessment over time and show the patterns and variations of the data. These can help identify and compare the changes or trends in a person's cognition and the factors that may influence them.
- **Statistics and algorithms:** These are mathematical and computational tools that can analyze and process the data of the cognitive assessment and calculate the measures and indicators of the changes or trends in a person's cognition, such as the rate, magnitude, and significance of the change. These can help quantify and validate the changes or trends in a person's cognition and the factors that may affect them.

Tracking changes should be done consistently and accurately, as cognitive impairment and dementia can have subtle and variable effects on a person's cognition and may not be noticeable or reliable in a single or isolated assessment. Tracking changes should also be done by a qualified, experienced professional who can interpret the data and provide feedback and guidance.

Cognitive assessment and tracking changes are essential for preserving cognition in patients with demyelinating diseases. By measuring and evaluating a person's cognitive abilities and functions and recording and analyzing the results over time, cognitive assessment and tracking changes can help diagnose and monitor cognitive impairment and dementia and provide the basis for treating and managing the symptoms.

Compensatory Techniques and Aids

Compensatory techniques and aids are strategies and devices to help patients with demyelinating diseases cope with their cognitive impairment and preserve their cognition. These techniques and aids can help patients compensate for their mental weaknesses, enhance their cognitive strengths, and improve their daily functioning and quality of life.

Some examples of compensatory techniques and aids are:

- **External memory aids:** These tools can help patients remember and organize information, such as calendars, planners, alarms, timers, notes, lists, labels, and apps. These aids can help patients keep track of their appointments, tasks, medications, and other important details.

- **Internal memory strategies:** These methods can help patients encode and retrieve information, such as mnemonics, associations, imagery, and repetition. These strategies can help patients improve their memory for names, faces, words, and numbers.

- **Attention and concentration techniques:** These can help patients focus and avoid distractions, such as setting goals, breaking down tasks, prioritizing, and eliminating noise and clutter. These techniques can help patients complete their tasks more efficiently and accurately.

- **Problem-solving and decision-making skills:** These skills can help patients analyze and resolve problems, such as defining the problem, generating alternatives, evaluating consequences, and choosing the best option. These skills can help patients cope with challenges and changes in their daily lives.

- **Communication and social skills:** These skills, such as listening, speaking, writing, and reading, can help patients interact and communicate with others. These skills can help patients express their needs and feelings, understand others, and maintain social relationships.

Compensatory techniques and aids can be learned and practiced with the help of a professional, such as a neuropsychologist, a speech therapist, or an occupational therapist, who can assess the patient's cognitive abilities and needs and provide individualized training and feedback. Compensatory techniques and aids can also be integrated into the patient's daily routine and environment and supported by the patient's family, friends, and caregivers, who can provide encouragement and assistance.

Maximizing Function Through Neuroplasticity

Neuroplasticity is the ability of the brain to change and adapt in response to experience, learning, and injury. Neuroplasticity can help patients with demyelinating diseases, such as multiple sclerosis, neuromyelitis optica, and chronic inflammatory demyelinating polyneuropathy, to preserve and improve their cognitive function and quality of life.

Maximizing function through neuroplasticity involves stimulating and challenging the brain in various ways, such as:

- Engaging in physical activity can improve blood flow, oxygen delivery, and nerve growth in the brain.

- Participating in cognitive rehabilitation can enhance memory, attention, problem-solving, and communication skills.
- Learning new skills or hobbies can increase the brain's plasticity and adaptability.
- Compensatory techniques and aids can help cope with cognitive impairment and improve daily functioning.
- Maintaining social and emotional well-being can reduce stress, loneliness, and depression and increase happiness and resilience.

Maximizing function through neuroplasticity requires motivation, effort, consistency, and the support and guidance of professionals, such as neurologists, neuropsychologists, physical therapists, occupational therapists, and speech therapists. These professionals can help assess the patient's cognitive abilities and needs and provide individualized training and feedback. Maximizing function through neuroplasticity is one of the options that can help patients with demyelinating diseases preserve their cognition and improve their quality of life.

Chapter 7

Creating Your Prevention Plan

Assessing Your Risk Factors

Assessing your risk factors is the first step in creating your prevention plan for demyelinating diseases. Risk factors are the conditions or behaviors that can increase your chances of developing a disease. By knowing your risk factors, you can take steps to reduce or eliminate them and lower your risk of demyelinating diseases.

Some of the risk factors for demyelinating diseases are:

- **Age:** The risk of demyelinating diseases increases with age, especially after 50 years old. Age-related changes in the brain, such as reduced blood flow, inflammation, and oxidative stress, can affect the structure and function of the myelin and the nerve cells.

- **Genetics:** Some genes can influence the risk of demyelinating diseases, either by increasing or decreasing it. For example, the HLA-DRB1 gene, which is involved in the immune system, has different variants that can affect the risk of multiple sclerosis, the most common demyelinating disease.

- **Family history:** Having a parent or sibling with a demyelinating disease can increase your risk of developing the same condition, especially if the onset was before 50 years old. This may be due to genetic or environmental factors, or both.

- **Infections:** Some viral or bacterial infections can trigger or worsen demyelination by causing inflammation or autoimmunity in the brain and spinal cord. Some infections linked to demyelinating diseases are Epstein-Barr virus, herpes simplex virus, varicella-zoster virus, and Mycoplasma pneumonia.

- **Autoimmunity:** Autoimmunity is when your immune system mistakenly attacks your tissues, such as myelin or nerve cells. Genetic, environmental, or hormonal factors or infections can cause autoimmunity. Some autoimmune diseases that can cause demyelination are lupus, Sjogren's syndrome, and sarcoidosis.

- **Lifestyle factors:** Some habits or behaviors can influence the risk of demyelinating diseases by protecting or harming the brain. These include smoking, alcohol consumption, physical activity, diet, vitamin D levels, stress management, and cognitive stimulation.

The risk factors for demyelinating diseases are not deterministic, meaning they do not guarantee that you will or will not develop a disease. They are probabilistic, meaning they can increase or decrease the likelihood of disease. Therefore, it is possible to prevent or delay demyelinating diseases by modifying some risk factors, especially lifestyle factors.

Setting Goals for Lifestyle, Diet, and Brain Health

Setting goals for lifestyle, diet, and brain health is an excellent way to improve your well-being and prevent or delay demyelinating diseases. Demyelinating diseases are conditions that cause damage to the myelin sheath that surrounds and protects the nerve fibers in the brain and spinal cord.

This can impair the communication between different brain regions and reduce the brain's plasticity and adaptability. This can also lead to the degeneration and death of nerve cells, which can cause irreversible brain damage and cognitive decline.

Some factors that can influence the risk of demyelinating diseases are age, genetics, family history, infections, autoimmunity, and lifestyle factors, such as smoking, alcohol consumption, physical activity, diet, vitamin D levels, stress management, and cognitive stimulation. Modifying some of these factors, especially lifestyle factors, can lower your risk of demyelinating diseases and protect your myelin and cognition.

To set goals for lifestyle, diet, and brain health, you can use the SMART goal framework, which stands for Specific, Measurable, Attainable, Relevant, and Time-bound. SMART goals can help you define what you want to do and how you will measure your progress. For example, if you want to improve your physical activity, a SMART goal could be:

- **Specific:** I want to walk for at least 30 minutes five days a week.
- **Measurable:** I will use a pedometer or an app to track my steps and time.
- **Attainable:** I will start with 10 minutes daily and gradually increase it to 30 minutes.
- **Relevant:** I want to improve my cardiovascular health, blood flow, and nerve growth in the brain.

- **Time-bound:** I will achieve this goal in the next two months.

You can set SMART goals for your lifestyle, diet, and brain health, such as eating more fruits and vegetables, quitting smoking, reducing stress, or learning a new skill. You can also consult your doctor or nutritionist for personalized advice and guidance. You can use online or paper journals, calendars, or apps to monitor your progress and hold yourself accountable. You can also seek support and feedback from your family, friends, or a group that can encourage and motivate you.

Developing A Schedule and Tracking Progress

Developing a schedule and tracking progress are essential steps for managing a project successfully. A schedule is a plan that outlines a project's tasks, resources, and deadlines. A progress tracker is a tool that monitors the performance and status of a project. These steps help you plan, execute, and control your project effectively.

To develop a schedule for your project, you can follow these steps:

- Define the scope and objectives of your project, and identify the deliverables and requirements.
- Break-down the work into smaller, more manageable tasks and group them into phases or stages.

- Estimate each task's duration, cost, and resource needs, and assign responsibilities to team members.

- Identify the dependencies and constraints among the tasks and sequence them logically.

- Create a timeline or a calendar that shows the project's start and end dates, milestones, and critical path.

- Review and adjust the schedule as needed, and get approval from the stakeholders.

To track the progress of your project, you can follow these steps:

- Define the metrics and indicators that measure the project's quality, time, and cost, and set the baseline and targets for each.

- Collect and record the data and information about the actual performance and status of the project, such as the completed tasks, the spent hours, and the incurred costs.

- Compare the actual and planned data and calculate the variance and deviation for each metric and indicator.

- Analyze the causes and effects of the variance and deviation, and identify the risks and issues that may affect the project.

- Report and communicate the progress and status of the project to the stakeholders and provide feedback and recommendations.

- Implement corrective and preventive actions to address the risks and issues, and update the schedule and the plan as needed.

Developing a schedule and tracking progress can help you manage your project efficiently and effectively. However, these steps can be complex, time-consuming, and require various tools and techniques. Therefore, it is advisable to use project management software, such as **Asana, Kissflow,** or **ProjectManager,** that can help you create and monitor your schedule and progress easily and accurately. These programs have features that allow you to:

- Visualize your project plan in standard, defined formats, such as Gantt charts, Kanban boards, or timelines.

- Schedule tasks and resources consistently and effectively, and link dependencies and constraints.

- Track information about your project's work, duration, and resource requirements, and generate reports and dashboards.

- Assign work, collaborate with team members, and communicate with stakeholders.

- Adjust and update your schedule, plan as needed, and implement changes and actions.

Working with Your Healthcare Team

Working with your healthcare team is key to managing your health and preventing or delaying demyelinating diseases. Demyelinating diseases are conditions that cause damage to the myelin sheath that surrounds and protects the nerve fibers in the brain and spinal cord. This can impair the communication between different brain regions and reduce the brain's plasticity and adaptability. This can also lead to the degeneration and death of nerve cells, which can cause irreversible brain damage and cognitive decline.

Your healthcare team may include various professionals, such as your general practitioner (GP), neurologist, neuropsychologist, physical therapist, occupational therapist, speech therapist, nutritionist, pharmacist, and nurse. Each can provide different services and support for your health and well-being, such as diagnosis, treatment, rehabilitation, education, and counseling.

To work effectively with your healthcare team, you can follow these tips:

- Communicate openly and honestly with your healthcare team, and share your medical history, symptoms, concerns, and goals.

- Ask questions, seek clarification if you do not understand something, and request written information or resources.
- Follow the instructions and prescriptions of your healthcare team, and report any changes or problems with your health or treatment.
- Give feedback, express your satisfaction or dissatisfaction with your healthcare team, and suggest any improvements or changes that you would like to see.
- Respect the expertise and opinions of your healthcare team, advocate for your needs and preferences, and seek a second opinion if necessary.
- Involve your family, friends, or caregivers in your healthcare, and ask them to accompany you to appointments or provide emotional and practical support.
- Give consent for your healthcare team to share information and coordinate your care, and appoint one healthcare professional, usually your GP, to oversee all your care.

Working with your healthcare team can help you manage your health and prevent or delay demyelinating diseases. By communicating and collaborating with your healthcare team, you can benefit from their knowledge and skills and improve your quality of life.

Conclusion

emyelinating diseases are conditions that cause damage to the myelin sheath that surrounds and protects the nerve fibers in the brain and spinal cord. This can impair the communication between different brain regions and reduce the brain's plasticity and adaptability. This can also lead to the degeneration and death of nerve cells, which can cause irreversible brain damage and cognitive decline.

There is no cure for demyelinating diseases, but there are treatments that can help manage the symptoms, modify the course of the disease, and improve the prognosis of the patients. However, these treatments are insufficient to restore the lost or damaged myelin and prevent the progressive neurodegeneration in these diseases.

Therefore, there is a great need for and interest in developing new therapies that promote remyelination and neuroprotection in demyelinating diseases. Remyelination is repairing or restoring the myelin sheath surrounding and protecting nerve fibers. Neuroprotection is the process of preventing or reducing the damage and degeneration of nerve cells. These therapies can improve the cognition and well-being of patients with demyelinating diseases.

New treatments and studies are trying to improve remyelination and neuroprotection in diseases that damage the myelin sheath. These include drugs, cell therapies, gene therapies, and electrical stimulation. These therapies and research are promising and innovative, but they are still in the early stages of development and face many challenges and limitations. Therefore, more research and clinical trials are needed to validate and optimize these therapies for the benefit of patients.

In addition to these therapies and research, some other strategies and interventions can help patients with demyelinating diseases preserve their cognition and improve their quality of life. These include lifestyle modifications, diet and nutrition, cognitive rehabilitation, compensatory techniques and aids, and cognitive assessment and tracking changes. These strategies and interventions can help patients cope with their cognitive impairment, enhance their cognitive strengths, and improve their daily functioning and well-being.

By following these strategies and interventions and working with your healthcare team, you can create your own prevention plan for demyelinating diseases. A prevention plan is a personalized and comprehensive plan that outlines the goals, actions, and resources that can help you protect your myelin and cognition. A prevention plan can help you reduce or eliminate your risk factors and lower your risk of demyelinating diseases.

Demyelinating diseases are severe and complex conditions that can affect your brain and spinal cord and cause cognitive impairment and decline. However, they are not inevitable or irreversible; there are ways to prevent or delay them. Learning about demyelinating diseases and preserving your myelin and cognition can improve your health and quality of life.

Thank you for reading this book, and I hope you found it informative and helpful.

I wish you all the best.

Appendix

References

1. Albrecht, P., Bouchachia, I., Goebels, N., Henke, N., Hucke, S., Issberner, A.,... & Wiendl, H. (2012). Effects of dimethyl fumarate on neuroprotection and immunomodulation. Journal of Neuroinflammation, 9(1), 1-8.
2. Campbell, G. R., Worrall, J. T., & Mahad, D. J. (2014). The central role of mitochondria in axonal degeneration in multiple sclerosis. Multiple Sclerosis Journal, 20(14), 1806-1813.
3. Cree, B. A., & Hauser, S. L. (2018). Treatment of multiple sclerosis: a review. American Journal of Medicine, 131(11), 1380–1383.

4. Dendrou, C. A., Fugger, L., & Friese, M. A. (2015). Immunopathology of multiple sclerosis. Nature Reviews Immunology, 15(9), 545-558.

5. Fitzner, D., & Simons, M. (2010). Myelin degeneration and its impact on axonal function and survival in a neurodegenerative disease multiple sclerosis model. Cellular and Molecular Life Sciences, 67(6), 991–1000.

6. Franklin, R.J., & Ffrench-Constant, C. (2008). Remyelination in the CNS: from biology to therapy. Nature Reviews Neuroscience, 9(11), 839-855.

7. Jakimovski, D., Ramanathan, M., Weinstock-Guttman, B., & Zivadinov, R. (2019). Lifestyle modulators of neurodegeneration: the role of nutrition in age-related neurodegenerative diseases. Aging research reviews, 50, 49–61.

8. Kremer, D., Göttle, P., Hartung, H. P., & Küry, P. (2016). Pushing forward: remyelination as the new frontier in CNS diseases. Trends in Neurosciences, 39(4), 246-263.

9. Stangel, M., & Hartung, H. P. (2002). Remyelinating strategies for the treatment of multiple sclerosis. Progress in Neurobiology, 68(5), 361-376.

10. Yamout, B., & Alroughani, R. (2018). Multiple sclerosis. Seminars in neurology, 38(02), 212-225.

Resources

<u>Organizations:</u>

- National Multiple Sclerosis Society - Information, support groups, and research updates for MS patients and caregivers
- The Myelin Repair Foundation - Nonprofit advocating and funding myelin repair research
- Alzheimer's Association - Resources for cognitive health, aging, and dementia prevention
- American Brain Foundation - Funding research and offering info on brain conditions

<u>Books:</u>

- Multiple Sclerosis: A Self-Care Guide to Wellness, by Nancy Holland and June Halper
- The Better Brain Solution by Steven Masley
- The End of Mental Illness, by Daniel G. Amen
- Healthy Brain, Happy Life by Wendy Suzuki
- The Brain That Changes Itself, by Norman Doidge

<u>Websites:</u>

- MSFocus - Latest MS news and research updates
- EverydayHealth - Articles on living with MS and brain health
- PsychologyToday - Cognitive health blog posts

- ALZConnected - Online community for dementia and cognitive care
- BrainHQ - Online brain training program by Posit Science

<u>Videos:</u>

- TED Talks on Neuroplasticity, Myelin, and MS
- YouTube channels by neurologists on healthy cognition
- webinars on nutrition for MS through organizations

www.ingramcontent.com/pod-product-compliance
Lightning Source LLC
Chambersburg PA
CBHW050852260726
48660CB00006B/2588